THE GLOBAL OCEAN

Written by **Rochelle Strauss**

Illustrated by **Natasha Donovan**

A collection of books that inform children about the world
and inspire them to be better global citizens

Kids Can Press

For Amy and Oliver, with all my heart. xo — R.S.

For Sky and Luna, my companions in adventure, who have spent countless hours by the sea with me — N.D.

ACKNOWLEDGMENTS

Thank you to the fantastic team at Kids Can Press, especially Stacey Roderick for your patience and thoughtful insights, and Marie Bartholomew for your incredible vision. A special thank you to Natasha Donovan for bringing my words to life so vividly. Thank you to Catherine Dorton for all the coffees, treats and the incredible support. Thank you to my family, who are the best cheerleaders out there! And a very special thank you to Nate and Maddie Willis, my wonderful beta readers.

Finally, I am truly grateful to the following amazing individuals who answered my myriad of questions and shared their knowledge: Rita Bell (Monterey Bay Aquarium), George Matsumoto (Monterey Bay Aquarium Research Institute), Susan Haynes (NOAA Ocean Exploration/Collabralink Technologies Inc.), Diz Glithero (Canadian Ocean Literacy Coalition), Nicole Straughan and Abigail Speck (Ocean Wise), A. E. Copenhaver, Susan Gesner, Sabrina Suluai-Mahuka, Isabel Gaoteote Halatuituia, Danika Strecko and Tami Lunsford.

Thank you also to the Ontario Arts Council for their financial support.

Published in Canada and the U.S. by Kids Can Press Ltd.
25 Dockside Drive, Toronto, ON M5A 0B5

Kids Can Press is a Corus Entertainment Inc. company

www.kidscanpress.com

The artwork in this book was rendered in pencil, Procreate, and Photoshop.
The text is set in Segaon.

Edited by Stacey Roderick
Designed by Marie Bartholomew

Printed and bound in Buji, Shenzhen, China, in 10/2021 by WKT Company

CM 22 0 9 8 7 6 5 4 3 2 1

FSC
www.fsc.org
MIX
Paper from
responsible sources
FSC® C010256

Library and Archives Canada Cataloguing in Publication

Title: The global ocean / written by Rochelle Strauss ; illustrated by Natasha Donovan.

Names: Strauss, Rochelle, 1967– | Donovan, Natasha, illustrator.

Series: CitizenKid.

Description: Series statement: CitizenKid | Includes index.

Identifiers: Canadiana 20210219904 | ISBN 9781525304910 (hardcover)

Subjects: LCSH: Ocean — Juvenile literature. | LCSH: Oceanography — Juvenile literature. | LCSH: Environmental sciences — Juvenile literature. | LCSH: Human ecology — Juvenile literature.

Classification: LCC GC21.5 .S77 2022 | DDC j551.46 — dc23

Kids Can Press gratefully acknowledges that the land on which our office is located is the traditional territory of many nations, including the Mississaugas of the Credit, the Anishnabeg, the Chippewa, the Haudenosaunee and the Wendat peoples, and is now home to many diverse First Nations, Inuit and Métis peoples.

We thank the Government of Ontario, through Ontario Creates; the Ontario Arts Council; the Canada Council for the Arts; and the Government of Canada for supporting our publishing activity.

CONTENTS

EARTH'S BEATING HEART

What if Earth had a beating heart that powered everything on the planet?

In a way, the global ocean is like Earth's heart.

When you look on a map of the world, you see five great oceans: the Atlantic Ocean, the Pacific Ocean, the Indian Ocean, the Arctic Ocean and the Southern Ocean (also called the Antarctic Ocean). But what you may not realize is that these oceans are all linked by a system of water that moves between them. So, these five oceans are actually connected to form one single circulating ocean — the global ocean.

This global ocean is Earth's most important feature. It moves heat, oxygen and nutrients around the planet, supporting all life on Earth, much like your heart pumps blood through your body to move oxygen and nutrients. It is also home to more species and more habitats than anywhere else on the planet. Its water shapes Earth's climate and influences its weather. The global ocean stores carbon dioxide from the atmosphere and supplies oxygen for us to breathe. It is also a source of food for many of Earth's inhabitants living in the ocean and on land. And for humans, it provides food, energy, minerals and transportation, as well as a place to play, explore and enjoy.

A healthy global ocean is what keeps the planet flourishing and sustains all life on Earth, just like the beat of your heart keeps you alive and well. But the global ocean is in trouble. Let's dive into the pages of this book to learn about the issues affecting the global ocean and what we can do to help it, and the planet, heal.

ABOUT THE GLOBAL OCEAN

Over 4.4 billion years ago, Earth cooled and water vapor, or gas, in the atmosphere condensed into rain. The rain fell for hundreds of years, filling the basins — large depressions in Earth's surface — that eventually became the global ocean. Today, the global ocean holds 97 percent of Earth's water. That's about 1 300 000 000 000 000 000 000 liters (352 000 000 000 000 000 000 gallons) of water!

The global ocean is where you'll find Earth's highest peaks, longest mountain ranges and deepest valleys. But perhaps its most significant feature is that it connects all water on Earth, not just ocean water. It does this in two ways: through the water cycle and through the flow of its currents.

The water cycle is the constant movement of water between the ocean, the land and Earth's atmosphere — the layers of gases around the planet. As warmed ocean water evaporates, pure water vapor rises into the sky. When the vapor cools, it condenses into tiny droplets and forms clouds that drift around the planet. Eventually the droplets get heavy enough to fall to Earth as rain, snow, sleet or hail, which then runs into lakes, rivers, streams and ponds. These bodies of water link together to form watersheds — systems of waterways that lead back to the global ocean.

In the ocean, currents are formed by wind patterns, gravity and the rotation of Earth.

Some currents flow across the ocean's surface, others deep beneath it, and some flow from the surface down to the deep and back up again. Gyres are currents that move in a circular pattern. The global ocean has five major gyres — the North Atlantic, South Atlantic, Indian, North Pacific and South Pacific. These gyres drive what scientists call the ocean conveyor belt — the currents that move water between the ocean's basins, controlling the temperature, amount of salt and flow of nutrients throughout the global ocean.

So, you see, thanks to the global ocean, Earth's water is always on the move — flowing between ocean basins, swirling up from the depths to the surface and back down again, and shifting between the ocean's surface and the atmosphere. All life relies on this constant circulation of water, just as you need your beating heart to keep the blood pumping through your body.

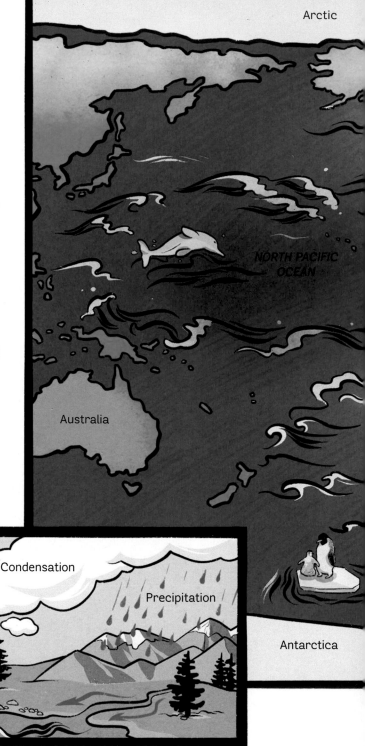

THE WATER CYCLE

Condensation

Precipitation

Evaporation

ARCTIC OCEAN

Asia

Europe

North America

NORTH ATLANTIC OCEAN

Africa

South America

INDIAN OCEAN

SOUTH ATLANTIC OCEAN

SOUTH PACIFIC OCEAN

SOUTHERN OCEAN

What can rubber ducks tell us about the flow of water in the global ocean? More than you might think! In 1992, a cargo ship was traveling across the Pacific Ocean from Hong Kong to Washington State. During a storm, one of the shipping containers it was carrying fell overboard, spilling nearly 28 000 rubber ducks (and other animal bath toys) into the ocean. Over the next 20 years, these rubber ducks (sometimes called "friendly floatees") washed up on shores all over the world — along the Pacific shorelines of Hawaii and Alaska, on Newfoundland's beaches on the eastern seaboard, and on the coasts of South America, Australia and Scotland. They were even found frozen into Arctic ice. The accidental spill turned into a real-time science experiment. Tracking the ducks allowed scientists to test their theories about the global ocean and learn more about ocean currents. Today, this story still reminds us how all the ocean basins are connected to form one global ocean.

Many animals that live in intertidal zones are adapted to live out of the water at low tide. Barnacles, for example, trap seawater in their closed shells, which keeps them from drying out as they wait for the tide to roll back in.

Some animals with the longest life spans live in the ocean. Among the record-setters are the volcano sponges of the Southern Ocean, which can live to be 15 000 years old!

Seagrass meadows are important habitats that help prevent erosion along the ocean shore. Seagrass roots trap sand and mud, keeping the currents from washing it away.

Hydrothermal vents are underwater geysers similar to hot springs on land. They release gases that can reach nearly 400° Celsius (752° Fahrenheit) — nearly as hot as the surface of Venus. Amazingly, marine animals such as feather duster worms and yeti crabs can be found living around these vents.

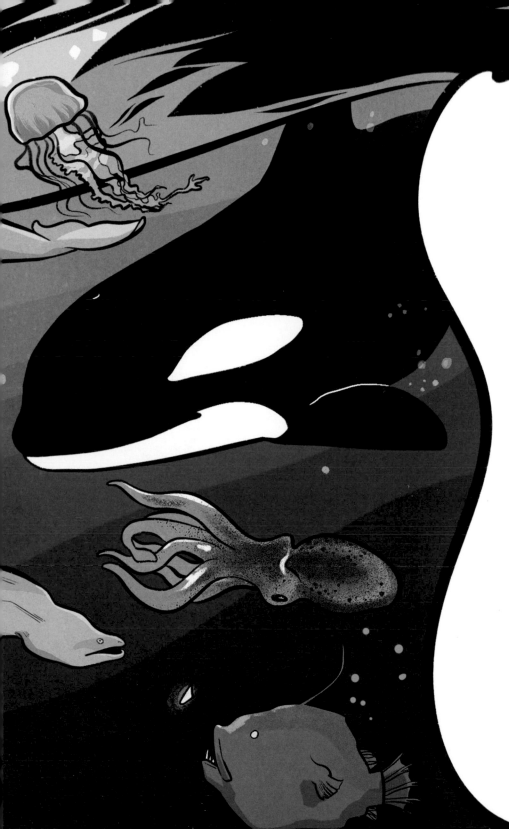

AN OCEAN OF DIVERSITY

The very first life-forms on Earth were ocean-dwelling microbes — tiny organisms that lived over four billion years ago. About 450 million years ago, plants were likely the first living things to wash ashore and begin life on land. Then 30 million years ago, prehistoric fishes left the oceans to live life on land. Every plant, animal and even bacteria species on Earth can trace its roots back to the ocean.

Today's global ocean is home to the greatest diversity of life on Earth. It's also home to the greatest number of living organisms on the planet. In fact, more than 50 percent of all life on Earth lives in the ocean. But the real number could be as high as 80 percent, because humans have explored only about 20 percent of the global ocean. Among the ocean's inhabitants are more than 242 000 different species of fish, invertebrates, plants, birds, reptiles and mammals — from the tiniest species, such as bacteria, to the largest mammal (and animal!) on the planet, the blue whale.

About 90 percent of Earth's habitats are also found in the global ocean. These habitats include the open ocean, hydrothermal vents, coral reefs, oyster reefs, seagrass meadows, kelp forests, saltwater marshes, mangrove forests, intertidal zones (where the ocean meets land) and estuaries (where rivers meet the sea). Many marine species are specially adapted to conditions in their habitat, such as water temperature, salt levels and light.

This incredible diversity of species and habitats in the ocean is very important for the overall health of the global ocean. That's because everything works together as part of an enormous, interconnected system. Without thriving habitats, species would struggle to survive. And since all species are part of food chains (who eats whom) and food webs (how food chains interconnect), a loss or change in the population of even one species will affect other species, including humans.

The Great Pacific Garbage Patch is a huge collection of floating trash found in the Pacific Ocean, between California and Hawaii. It's often referred to as a "plastic soup" because most of the garbage swirls beneath the ocean's surface.

ROUGH WATERS

Though we may not realize it, many human activities are having an impact on the health of the global ocean.

The burning of fossil fuels, such as coal, gasoline and oil, releases a gas called carbon dioxide into the atmosphere, causing Earth's climate to change. And as the global ocean absorbs more and more carbon dioxide from the atmosphere, the chemistry, or makeup, of the ocean water is changing. Plastics, chemicals and other debris dumped or washed into the ocean are endangering marine species and destroying ocean habitats. Human demand for fish is draining the ocean of fish and threatening natural food chains. And many coastal species are losing their habitats to buildings, roads and expanding cities.

Each of these issues causes damage on its own, but when combined they put even more stress on the global ocean. We are already seeing signs of this stress. But by studying these issues and their symptoms, scientists are learning more about the serious problems human activities are causing for the ocean and for the planet. With this knowledge, we can make plans and take action to help make the global ocean healthy again.

RIPPLE OF CHANGE!

In 2008, the United Nations officially declared June 8 World Oceans Day. Every year on that day, cities around the world host events such as cleanups, art shows and festivals that raise awareness and inspire people and governments to protect the global ocean. The World Oceans Day organization also has a Youth Advisory Council made up of people ages 16 to 22 from around the world that helps plan year-round actions.

CHANGING CLIMATE, CHANGING OCEAN

You might be surprised to learn that the global ocean plays an important role in shaping Earth's climate, including its average yearly temperatures, annual rainfall and the number of storms from year to year. And that, in turn, Earth's climate also has a powerful effect on the global ocean.

The ocean helps shape the climate by attracting energy from the sun and absorbing heat from the atmosphere, which warms its water — especially near the tropics and equator. The ocean conveyor belt moves the warm water from the equator to the North and South Poles and brings cold water from the poles back to the equator. As part of the water cycle, some of this warm water evaporates as it travels, putting heat and moisture into the air. The combination of the moving ocean water and the water cycle maintains Earth's temperature and drives rainfall patterns and storms.

But as we depend more and more on fossil fuels, humans are also having an effect on Earth's climate. Fossil fuels are burned with most car rides, with the flick of a light switch and to heat many homes. Factories burn these fuels to make products such as clothing and electronics, and planes, trucks and trains burn them shipping those products to us. Burning more fossil fuels means more and more carbon dioxide is released into the atmosphere. Some carbon dioxide in the atmosphere happens naturally, but the extra amounts released by human activity are creating a barrier of gases around Earth that is trapping heat and warming the planet.

Since the global ocean absorbs about 80 to 90 percent of the heat in the atmosphere, a warmer Earth will mean higher water temperatures, too. And as the ocean heats up, it affects the climate and weather. For instance, warmer water along the eastern coast of North America can bring harsher hurricanes. Scientists predict that the warmer water may also slow down ocean currents, which would change temperature and weather patterns around the world. Summers in Europe would become colder, while the tropics might experience different rainfall patterns.

So you see, it is all interconnected. Earth's changing climate is warming the global ocean, and rising ocean temperatures are affecting the climate. These changes will have a huge impact on all life on Earth, as sea levels rise and the makeup of the water changes.

Climate change is warming Arctic air faster than in other parts of the planet, causing sea ice to melt. As the ice disappears, there is more open ocean to absorb heat, which warms the water. The warmer water then causes even more sea ice to melt.

RiPPLE OF CHANGE!

Many governments have signed the Paris Agreement, a worldwide commitment to tackle the climate crisis. Some of the countries are looking at ways to use renewable energy, such as solar and wind energy, instead of burning fossil fuels. Morocco, for example, has the world's largest solar farm and the country is aiming for more than half of their energy to be renewable by 2030. And Scotland may soon be powered entirely by renewable energy!

WARMING WATERS

As the global ocean warms, its water expands and takes up more space. This causes water levels to rise. Additionally, as Earth warms, glaciers on land melt, adding to the rising sea levels. These higher water levels are causing flooding along the ocean's shorelines. Some cities at the ocean's edge, as well as island countries, may slowly begin to vanish beneath the sea. Rising water could also destroy entire coastal ecosystems, such as mangrove forests, estuaries and wetlands, and that loss of habitat would threaten countless marine species.

In addition to a loss of or change to their habitats, warming water will also mean other challenges for marine species. For example, they might starve if their food sources — whether plant, animal or microorganism — cannot survive in the higher temperatures. And while some species may be able to migrate, many others cannot.

For example, some species of kelp thrive only in cooler water. They can't move because they are rooted to the seafloor. These kelp forests are not only home to an incredible diversity of marine life, but they also absorb carbon dioxide and produce some of the oxygen we breathe.

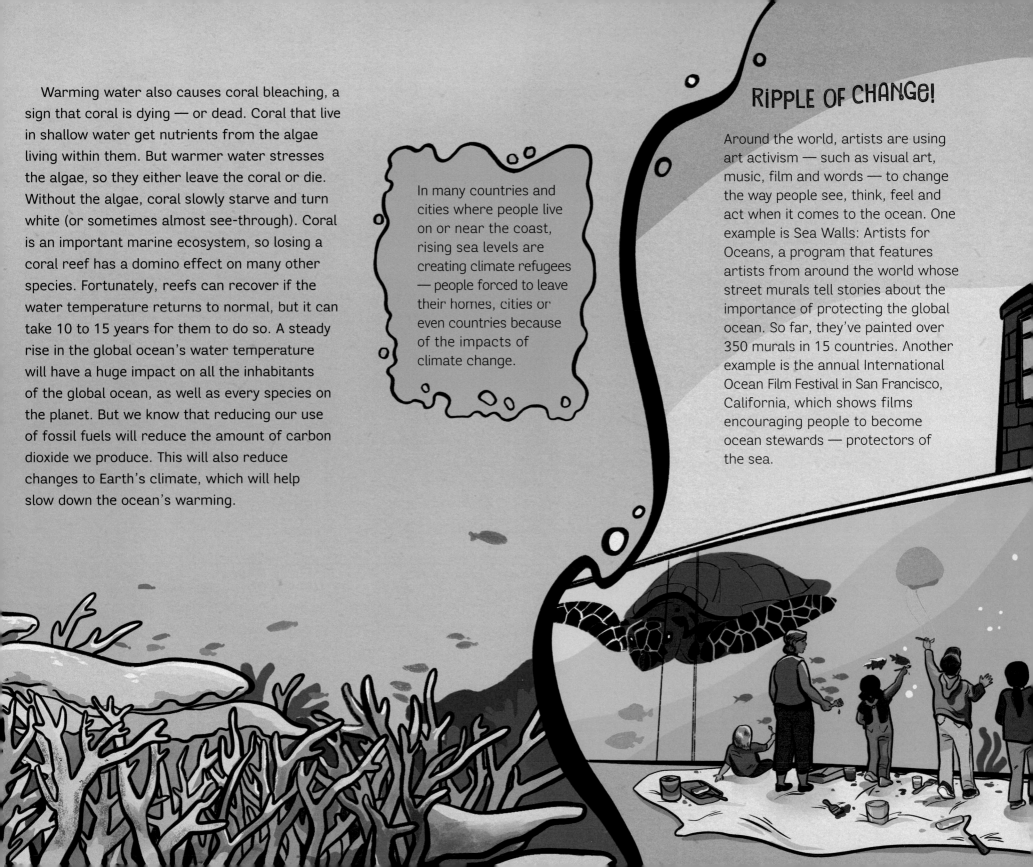

Warming water also causes coral bleaching, a sign that coral is dying — or dead. Coral that live in shallow water get nutrients from the algae living within them. But warmer water stresses the algae, so they either leave the coral or die. Without the algae, coral slowly starve and turn white (or sometimes almost see-through). Coral is an important marine ecosystem, so losing a coral reef has a domino effect on many other species. Fortunately, reefs can recover if the water temperature returns to normal, but it can take 10 to 15 years for them to do so. A steady rise in the global ocean's water temperature will have a huge impact on all the inhabitants of the global ocean, as well as every species on the planet. But we know that reducing our use of fossil fuels will reduce the amount of carbon dioxide we produce. This will also reduce changes to Earth's climate, which will help slow down the ocean's warming.

In many countries and cities where people live on or near the coast, rising sea levels are creating climate refugees — people forced to leave their homes, cities or even countries because of the impacts of climate change.

RIPPLE OF CHANGE!

Around the world, artists are using art activism — such as visual art, music, film and words — to change the way people see, think, feel and act when it comes to the ocean. One example is Sea Walls: Artists for Oceans, a program that features artists from around the world whose street murals tell stories about the importance of protecting the global ocean. So far, they've painted over 350 murals in 15 countries. Another example is the annual International Ocean Film Festival in San Francisco, California, which shows films encouraging people to become ocean stewards — protectors of the sea.

SINKING THE CARBON SINK

As well as higher water temperatures, there is another serious symptom of climate change harming the health of the global ocean: acidification. Acidification is a chemical change in the ocean's water that causes the water to become more acidic. Although it's not something you would notice when you go for a swim, a more acidic ocean *will* affect all life in the ocean and may even make it unlivable for some sea life.

But how does climate change cause ocean acidification? By adding more carbon to the ocean. It's important to understand that Earth is home to many "carbon sinks," which store carbon dioxide. These sinks include mangrove forests, tropical rainforests and seagrass meadows. Their plants remove carbon dioxide from the atmosphere and store it away in their roots, stems and leaves. But the *largest* carbon sink on Earth is the global ocean. Its water takes in about a third of all the carbon dioxide in the atmosphere! So, the more carbon dioxide human activities create, the more the ocean has to absorb. It's this added carbon dioxide that is making the ocean more acidic.

Many species will be affected by ocean acidification, but the species that may struggle the most are the ones with shells or exoskeletons, such as oysters, mussels, sea stars and lobsters. These animals need a mineral found in the ocean called calcium carbonate to build their shells, but acidic water dissolves calcium carbonate, which means there is less available for shell building. Oysters, for example, do most of their growing and shell building within the first 48 hours of life, and acidic water may eat away at the shells faster than they can form. Acidic water also breaks down existing shells and exoskeletons in animals, so even adult shellfish species are at risk.

The health of the global ocean depends on a rich diversity of species. Many of the animals most threatened by acidification are at the bottom of ocean food chains. Since these food chains (and the food webs they create) connect all marine species, changes to the ocean's chemistry threatens *all* creatures in the global ocean.

The global ocean currently absorbs about 20 million tonnes (22 million tons) of carbon dioxide per day. That's about 24 times the weight of the Golden Gate Bridge in San Francisco, California.

RIPPLE OF CHANGE!

Less carbon dioxide in the air means less in the ocean. That's why many countries are looking for alternative ways to power their vehicles — and not just cars and buses. For example, after launching its first electric ferry in 2015, Norway is aiming to have two-thirds of its fleet of passenger ferries powered by electricity by 2030. And in 2018, the Netherlands began using electric boats to carry cargo through its canals.

17

A SEA OF TRASH

Every year, *billions* of kilograms of pollution find their way into the ocean. Ocean pollution can be many different things: garbage, abandoned fishing gear, chemicals, pesticides and oil. And it comes from many sources. Trash from landfills and dumps can be blown into nearby rivers and streams that eventually lead to the ocean. Rain and melting snow can wash trash and chemicals, such as fertilizers, detergents, gasoline and road salt, into local waterways that lead to the ocean, too. Sometimes garbage, including chemical waste, is intentionally dumped into waterways and oceans. Accidental oil spills also pollute the ocean.

Each type of pollution causes a different problem for the global ocean. Garbage can sink to the ocean floor and damage habitats or wash ashore and destroy animal nesting sites. Spilled chemicals, such as oil, can coat an animal's skin, fur or feathers, making it harder for them to swim or even breathe. And if eaten, pollution can poison animals, making them very sick or, worse, killing them.

Maybe surprisingly, one of the deadliest forms of pollution for ocean life is something called ghost gear — lost or discarded nets, lines, traps and other fishing equipment. An estimated 640 000 tonnes (700 000 tons) of fishing gear are lost or left behind in the ocean *every* year. That's equal to the weight of about 3500 blue whales!

Ghost gear is dangerous for many reasons. Animals such as turtles, sharks, dolphins, whales and even seabirds get tangled in lost nets and lines, often never escaping. In fact, over 300 000 whales and dolphins get caught in ghost gear every year. Long after being lost, crab pots and other kinds of traps can keep on catching and killing marine life. And important habitats, such as coral reefs and kelp forests, are also damaged by the weight of lost and discarded fishing gear.

Ocean pollution, in all its forms, harms many of the marine species and habitats the global ocean needs to keep thriving. But there's one type of pollution that may be having the greatest impact on ocean health — plastic!

RiPPLE OF CHANGE!

The Global Ghost Gear Initiative (GGGI) is a group of governments, businesses (including from the fishing industry), community groups and individuals working together to remove ghost gear from the ocean. Among the countries involved are Belgium, Canada, the Dominican Republic, the Netherlands, New Zealand, Norway, Palau, Panama, Samoa, Sweden, Tonga, Tuvalu, the United Kingdom and Vanuatu. The collected ghost gear is recycled into products such as skateboards, knapsacks, sunglasses and running shoes!

Even noise and light pollute the global ocean. Underwater sounds from ships make it harder for sea animals to communicate. And artificial lights along the shorelines are a challenge for animals at night. For instance, lights along beaches and docks make it hard for newly hatched sea turtles to find their way to the sea.

THE PLASTIC PROBLEM

Look around. How many things do you see that are made of plastic? Plastic is one of the most widely used materials on Earth. It also makes up about *80 percent* of the trash found in the global ocean.

Plastic doesn't decompose, and many plastic items cannot be recycled. Like other garbage, it often ends up in the ocean. Over time, the sun, water and waves break the plastic down into tiny pieces called microplastics (pieces smaller than plankton) and pieces even thousands of times smaller, called nanoplastics. But no matter how small the pieces get, the plastic will always be there.

One big problem with plastic pollution is that marine animals often mistake it for food or sometimes swallow it accidentally. A floating plastic bag can look like a jellyfish to a hungry sea turtle. Fish may think microplastic pieces are the eggs they eat. Filter feeders, such as whale sharks, may accidentally eat plastic with their food. And it's estimated that nearly 90 percent of all seabirds have eaten plastic at some point in their lives. Because plastic cannot be digested, it makes animals feel too full to eat real food or it damages their digestive systems. The chemicals in the plastic can also poison animals. And when a predator eats an

animal that has eaten plastic, the poisons are passed along, all the way up the food chain.

Plastic also creates other hazards for ocean life. Larger plastic objects can damage or smother marine plants and habitats. Animals get tangled up in plastic debris, making it difficult or impossible for them to eat, swim or escape predators. And when young animals are unable to free themselves, the plastic may start to cut into them or even strangle them as they grow.

There isn't a single marine species or habitat that escapes the impact of plastic pollution. But plastic pollution, and, in fact, all pollution, is an issue that we can solve.

RiPPLE OF CHANGE!

In 2002, Bangladesh became the first country to ban single-use plastic bags. Since then, over 40 countries, including Rwanda, Italy, South Africa, the Netherlands, China, Israel and France, have either banned or discouraged single-use plastics, and many other countries and cities will soon join them. Kenya has some of the strictest laws against single-use plastic bags — it's illegal to use, make or sell them.

Did you know that many common human-made fabrics, such as nylon and polyester, contain plastic? This means that with every load of laundry, as many as 17 million tiny plastic fibers may get washed down the drain. Most of these fibers end up in waterways that eventually flow into the ocean.

21

A FISHING FRENZY

Did you know that fish is the primary food source for nearly one-third of the people on Earth? And as the world's population continues to grow, the need for fish is higher than ever. The impact of meeting the demand for fish is being felt throughout the global ocean.

Overfishing is just one consequence of the world's enormous demand for fish. Because of new technologies and ways of fishing, more fish can be caught, and they can be caught faster than ever before. This means that fish species aren't given the chance to grow, reproduce or rebuild their numbers. New technology also makes it easier to track and catch fish in deeper waters, which also leads to overfishing.

Another problem with today's fishing practices is bycatch — animals that are caught accidentally. How does that happen? Imagine a net designed to catch a particular kind of fish. But other animals that are the same size as that fish or bigger also get caught in the net and hauled onboard with the rest of the catch. They usually die as a result. Every year, billions of unwanted fish, sea turtles, rays, birds and even dolphins and whales are victims of bycatch.

Some fishing practices are also destroying important marine habitats. In dredging, for example, a large metal scoop is dragged across the ocean floor to catch bottom-dwelling animals, such as crabs, scallops and clams. In the process, the seafloor is damaged and other species are harmed or killed. In bottom trawling, large nets with heavy weights are pulled across the seafloor to catch fish such as flounder, and in the process, they destroy everything in their path, including coral and oyster reefs. But because the demand for these species is high, these practices are still used even though they cause serious habitat damage.

With so much of the world's population dependent on fish for food, banning fishing isn't possible. But sustainable fishing offers a way to protect the global ocean. Sustainable fishing means leaving enough fish in the ocean to allow fish populations to recover and rebuild. It also means using fishing methods that lower the risk of bycatch and reduce habitat destruction.

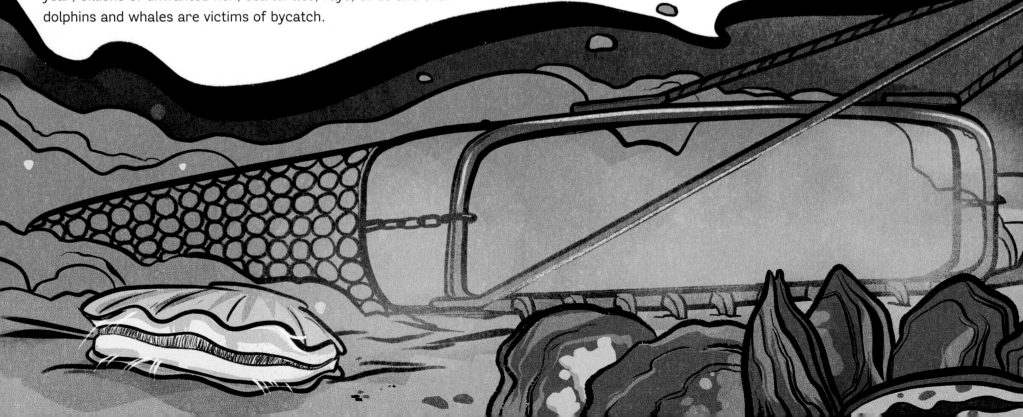

Overfishing of one species affects other species, too. In the Shetland Islands of Scotland, puffins mainly eat fish called sand eels. When sand eels were overfished, the puffins lost an important source of food and their population dropped.

RIPPLE OF CHANGE!

If you or your family love to eat seafood, there are organizations that can help you make ocean-friendly choices when shopping or eating out. Monterey Bay Aquarium's Seafood Watch and the Ocean Wise Seafood Program are two programs that provide lists of fish that are caught using sustainable practices, ensuring fish populations aren't being overfished.

SUSTAINABLY CAUGHT

A COST TO THE COASTLINE

Humans are changing the natural landscape of the global ocean's shores and coastlines all around the world. Coastal wetlands are being taken over and used for farming, aquaculture (such as fish and shrimp farming) and building developments, including hotels, resorts and homes.

Seagrass meadows and mangrove forests are just two examples of important coastal habitats that are being seriously affected by human activity. Nearly 30 percent of all the seagrass meadows in the world have been destroyed by construction over the last hundred years. This loss has many effects since seagrass roots help keep the seabed from washing away; seagrass itself cleans water by catching contaminants; and like other plants, seagrass collects and stores carbon dioxide. As well, thousands of marine species live, feed and raise their young in seagrass meadows. Mangrove forests are also significant carbon sinks and provide a habitat for thousands of marine species, yet they are being cut down to make room for farmland, aquaculture and industrial areas.

Whole cities have been built all along the global ocean's coast, including Hong Kong, Sydney and New York. Concrete or stone seawalls, breakwaters and jetties have been built to protect these coastal cities from rising tides and storms. But these "hardened" shorelines have changed and destroyed the natural habitats along these parts of the coast.

When we lose coastal habitats, we lose species diversity. Paving over breeding and feeding grounds not only puts the survival of many aquatic animals at risk, but it also threatens the animals that feed on them. And since many habitats include trees and other plants, losing these habitats also means losing important carbon sinks. All this has an impact on the health of the global ocean. Thankfully, these losses can be prevented if we make the commitment to protect and restore marine habitats.

RIPPLE OF CHANGE!

Seagrass meadows are important habitats and carbon sinks, which is why there are many conservation groups and researchers working to protect and regrow them. For example, the Seagrass Ocean Rescue Project in Wales has hundreds of volunteers, including children, stuffing seed bags and planting them in areas where seagrass has been lost. Their goal is to plant one million seeds to help replace lost seagrass meadows.

One hectare (2.5 acres) of seagrass can store about twice as much carbon dioxide as the same area of rain forest. And seagrass meadows absorb carbon dioxide about 35 times faster, too!

WAVES OF CHANGE

The global ocean is much more than the water you see. It is the beating heart that supports all life on Earth. It's the air we breathe, the climate we live in and home to the richest diversity of life on the planet. We need the global ocean to be healthy so that it can keep supporting *every* living species on Earth, including us.

But as we have seen, the global ocean is facing some serious challenges that are affecting its overall health.

Thankfully, many governments, Indigenous communities, businesses, organizations, scientists, artists, activists, teachers and young people are taking charge and leading the way to conserve and restore the global ocean. And what started out as a few ripples is growing into bigger waves of change!

This global action is necessary to give the ocean the support it needs to heal. Here are a few examples of the waves of change happening around the world.

Climate Action

Over the years, many groups have tackled the issue of climate change, and the movement continues to grow. As part of the Global Climate Strike in September 2019, more than seven million people worldwide walked out of school and work, filling streets and parks in protest. And young people from around the world, including youth climate activists like Komal Karishma Kumar (Fiji), Autumn Peltier (Canada), Bruno Rodriguez (Argentina), Greta Thunberg (Sweden) and others, continue to speak out, demanding governments and businesses make changes that address the climate crisis.

Cleaning the Coasts

Shoreline cleanups are one way to keep garbage from entering the ocean and to protect important shoreline habitats. Ocean Conservancy International hosts a yearly International Coastal Cleanup Day on the third Saturday of September. Each year, millions of volunteers from around the world pick up the garbage littering their local beaches and clogging waterways. In 2018, over one million volunteers collected more than 10 million kilograms (over 23 million pounds) of trash in total. That's about the same weight as 550 whale sharks (the largest fish in the sea)! Most of the garbage was single-use plastic, such as straws, wrappers, bottles and cigarette butts (yes, there's plastic in cigarette butts). That year included some surprises, too, such as a video game console, a chandelier and a vacuum cleaner.

Finding Solutions to the Plastic Problem

Around the world, designers, scientists and innovators are working together to come up with solutions to the plastic problem, such as making new materials to use instead of plastic. To replace thousands of plastic water bottles at the London Marathon in England, runners were given edible water pods made from seaweed extracts. They simply popped the pods into their mouths and chewed on the pod to release the water. And instead of all those pesky plastic stickers on fruits and vegetables, the use of laser "labels" that remove skin color from fruits and vegetables is being tested. Young people are getting involved in researching solutions, too. British university student Lucy Hughes won the 2019 James Dyson Award by developing a biodegradable plastic from fish waste, such as skin and scales. The plastic can be tossed into household compost bins after it's used.

Reducing Bycatch

To reduce the amount of bycatch, new techniques and gear are being designed and used by fishers around the world. For example, hooks used on some types of fishing lines are being redesigned to stop sea turtles from being caught. Sound is being tested to try to scare animals, such as small whales and dolphins, away from fishing nets. And an invention called the turtle excluder device (TED) protects turtles from shrimp trawlers: its grid of metal bars is attached to the nets to prevent bigger animals, such as turtles, from accidentally being caught.

Marine Habitat Conservation

Marine Protected Areas (MPAs) are like national parks — except that they are in the water! MPAs protect ecosystems, habitats and species, helping areas recover from the effects of habitat loss, overfishing and pollution. There is a global goal to have 30 percent of the global ocean covered by MPAs by 2030. One of the largest MPAs is the Papahānaumokuākea Marine National Monument off the coast of Hawaii in the United States. It's bigger than all the national parks in America put together! And one of the newest MPAs is Tallurutiup Imanga, a National Marine Conservation Area established on an area of traditional Inuit coastal land in the northeastern region of Nunavut, Canada. Its creation was led by the Qikiqtani Inuit Association, and Inuit Traditional Knowledge will help guide how to manage and protect this conservation area.

Finding Your Wave

No matter where you live, you can help the global ocean, too. All you need to do is start your own wave! If each of us takes even one action, we will soon be riding the waves of change needed to make sure Earth's heart is healthy.

What action (or actions) will you take to help heal the global ocean? Here are just a few ideas to help you start your wave:

• Learn more, and share what you know. The more you know about the ocean, the more likely you are to want to take action to protect it. And make sure you pass it on! Encouraging others to think about the ocean will help create a more powerful wave of change.

• Find a way to think about the ocean every day, so that you are always reminded that it is an important part of our lives — no matter where you live. Put up pictures of the ocean on your walls, fill a jar with beach sand, listen to recordings of ocean waves or even livestream the sound of whales calling in the wild.

• Shop wisely. Try not to buy things you don't need or things that you'll throw away after one or two uses. Before you buy something, think first if it can be reused or repurposed when you're done with it. And when something breaks, try to fix it rather than throwing it out or replacing it. The less that ends up in the wastebasket, the less garbage there will be in the ocean.

• Say no to single-use plastic! Bring reusable bags and containers to the grocery store or when you get takeout food. Try to remember to BYOC — bring your own cutlery — to school, camp and even fast-food restaurants. Use reusable water bottles and mugs when you're out. And did you know you can get reusable, compostable beeswax-based food wraps to use instead of plastic wrap?

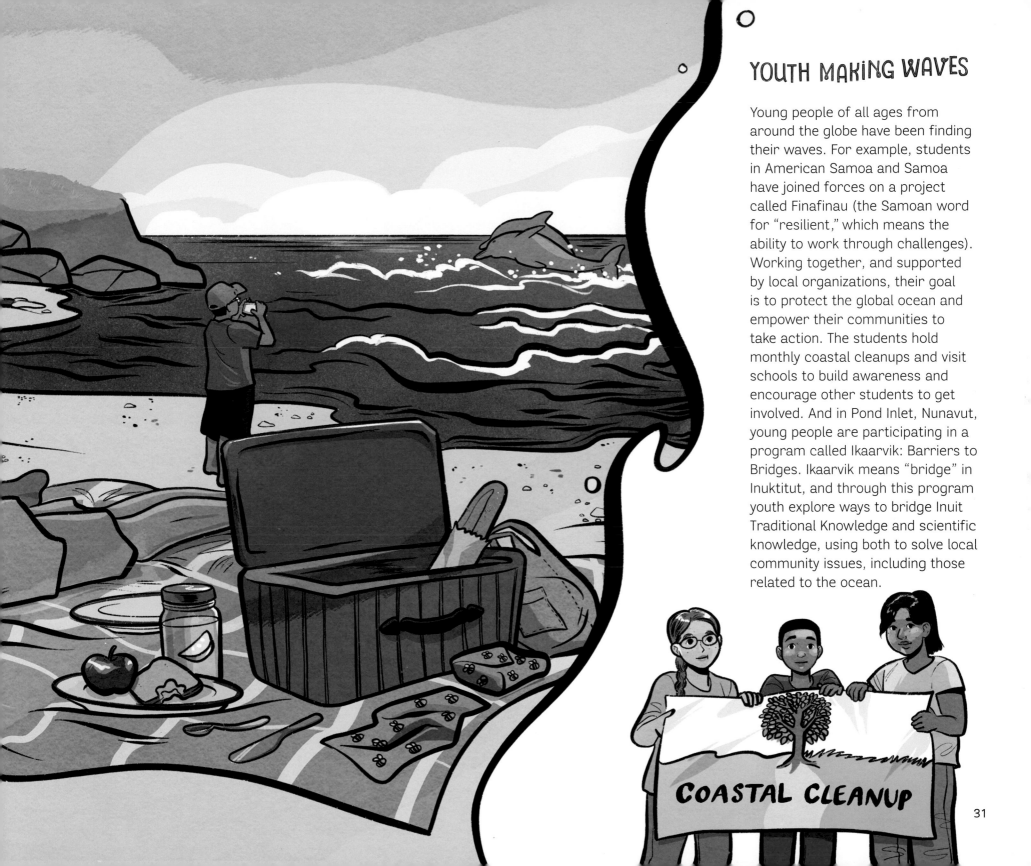

YOUTH MAKING WAVES

Young people of all ages from around the globe have been finding their waves. For example, students in American Samoa and Samoa have joined forces on a project called Finafinau (the Samoan word for "resilient," which means the ability to work through challenges). Working together, and supported by local organizations, their goal is to protect the global ocean and empower their communities to take action. The students hold monthly coastal cleanups and visit schools to build awareness and encourage other students to get involved. And in Pond Inlet, Nunavut, young people are participating in a program called Ikaarvik: Barriers to Bridges. Ikaarvik means "bridge" in Inuktitut, and through this program youth explore ways to bridge Inuit Traditional Knowledge and scientific knowledge, using both to solve local community issues, including those related to the ocean.

COASTAL CLEANUP

• Use cold water for laundry. When material is washed in hot water, the fabric breaks down faster. With cold water, fewer plastic fibers get washed away and end up in the waterways and eventually the ocean. Looking for clothing made from plastic-free cotton or bamboo material is a great idea, too.

• Reduce how much carbon dioxide you produce in your daily activities. There are lots of small things you can do that will help. For example, try walking or biking instead of driving. Take public transportation whenever possible. Remember to power off electronics, such as your computer and gaming console, and turn off lights when you don't need them.

• Help clean up beaches and shorelines. Plan or join a cleanup of a shoreline or anyplace where water meets land. It can be a family outing, a class trip or part of something even bigger. Many organizations run events all year long — do a bit of research and see what might already be planned near you.

• Be an art activist. Use your art, photos, videos, music or writing to share ocean stories and raise awareness about ocean issues. Invite your friends to do the same. Host an ocean-themed art show at your school or local community center.

• Celebrate World Oceans Day every June 8. Organize events at your school or in your community to focus attention on the issues facing the global ocean. You might even consider joining the World Oceans Day Youth Council one day.

• Use your voice! Think about an ocean issue that's important to you and speak up! Become a champion for ocean-friendly changes at your school, or suggest changes to businesses in your neighborhood. You could even take your ideas to the decision makers in your community.

NOTE TO TEACHERS, PARENTS AND GUARDIANS

"Knowing is the key to caring, and with caring there is hope that people will be motivated to take positive actions."
— *Sylvia Earle, oceanographer, explorer, author and activist*

OCEAN LITERACY

As teachers, parents and guardians, we can play an important role in encouraging young people to become stewards of the global ocean, Earth's beating heart. Guiding them in this journey means helping them acquire ocean literacy, an understanding of the influence the ocean has on us and the influence that we have on the ocean. Ocean literacy is key to helping us understand our complex relationship with the global ocean. It is founded on seven key principles, or concepts, that have been explored throughout this book. They are:

1. Earth has one big ocean with many features.

2. The ocean and life in the ocean shape Earth's features.

3. The ocean is a major influence on climate and weather.

4. The ocean made Earth habitable.

5. The ocean supports a great diversity of life and ecosystems.

6. The ocean and humans are inextricably interconnected.

7. The ocean is largely unexplored.

Around the world, we are seeing how activism and innovation aren't just for adults: children and teens are speaking out and sharing their visions for the future. They are also taking the lead in developing new ideas to support ocean sustainability and conservation. You can help the children and young people in your life express their ideas, and empower them to create, innovate or act. Encourage them to explore the ocean through their stories, songs, videos, poems and art. Nurture budding innovators as they experiment and investigate ideas that might protect the ocean. Support young activists as they take action.

AT SCHOOL

Ocean learning shouldn't just happen in science class! Infuse the ocean across all subjects. Study the significance of the ocean in different cultures and throughout history. Read stories, poems or essays that relate to the ocean in some way. Fill math homework with ocean-themed problems or run hackathons to code programs that address ocean conservation. Use the ocean as the foundation for media studies assignments; include ocean sounds in music class; explore the ocean through art. Start an ocean club, host an ocean innovation science fair, celebrate World Oceans Day or organize a shoreline cleanup. There are so many ways to bring the global ocean into each school day and across all subjects.

AT HOME

One of the most important steps you can take at home is to bring the ocean into your daily lives. Being at the ocean is one way to connect, but that is not always so easy to do, or even possible. Instead, you can fill your home with stories, images and sounds of the ocean. Also, be curious! As a family, read books, watch movies, visit websites or listen to podcasts to learn more. Explore all the ways your daily activities are connected to the ocean and, wherever possible, make changes that support ocean sustainability. For example, consider doing a plastic audit of your home as a family project: record all the places and ways you use plastic, then brainstorm how to reduce your plastic footprint. You might even encourage your family to take part in Plastic Free July, a global movement in which people around the world reduce their use of single-use plastic for the month of July. Who knows, the new habits your family develops in that one month may last all year long!

WANT MORE?

There are many organizations and resources that can support you, your family and your classroom in building your ocean literacy. Here are just a few to help you continue your ocean exploration:

- **Canadian Network for Ocean Education** http://oceanliteracy.ca/
- **Canadian Ocean Literacy Coalition** https://colcoalition.ca/
- **IOC-UNESCO Ocean Literacy Portal** https://oceanliteracy.unesco.org/
- **Mission Blue** https://mission-blue.org/
- **Monterey Bay Aquarium** https://www.montereybayaquarium.org/
- **Monterey Bay Aquarium Research Institute** https://www.mbari.org/
- **National Marine Educators Association** https://www.marine-ed.org/
- **National Oceanic and Atmospheric Association** https://www.noaa.gov/
- **Ocean Conservation Trust** https://oceanconservationtrust.org/
- **Ocean Wise** https://ocean.org/

INDEX